A Little Italian Cookbook

Anna Del Conte

ILLUSTRATED BY CARL MELAGARI

First published in 1990 by

The Appletree Press Ltd

19-21 Alfred Street

BELFAST BT2 8DL

Tel: ++44 (0) 1232 243074

Fax: ++44 (0) 1232 246756

email: frontdesk@appletree.ie

website address: www.irelandseye.com

Olivio is a registered trademark.

A Little Italian Cookbook

9 8 7 6 5 4

Introduction

To represent the wealth and variety of Italian cooking, I have chosen recipes to typify the cuisines of each region. They vary from the rich, dark Beef Braised in Barolo wine, from Piedmont, to the Sicilian Pasta with Fresh Sardines, redolent of the fresh aromas of the Mediterranean. They are all traditional dishes, all still made in their place of origin, though in as many variations as there are cooks. These are my versions, and I hope they will inspire you to try them in your own kitchen. Start by following the recipes precisely, then once you have learned how to cook *all'Italiana,* you can add your own personal touch.

A word on ingredients. The secret of Italian cooking lies in making the best possible use of first-class foodstuffs, with very few added sauces or garnishes. For this reason I advise you to buy only the best ingredients and, whenever possible, Italian products rather than local substitutes.

A note on measures

All ingredients are given in imperial, metric and American measures. Although the difference between versions is small, you should use the same kind of measure throughout any one recipe. In the volume measurements given for American readers, a tablespoon is level and a cup is equal to 8 fluid ounces.

All the recipes are for 4 persons unless otherwise stated.

Zuppa alla Pavese

This nourishing consommé comes from Pavia, in southern Lombardy. The soup is said to have earned royal approval when, in 1525, a local woman served it to Francis I of France after the battle of Pavia against Charles V.

1¾ pints / 1 litre / 4 cups homemade stock
2 oz / 50g / ¼ cup butter
4 slices good-quality white bread
4 eggs
4 tbsp freshly grated Parmesan cheese
salt and freshly ground black pepper

Bring the stock to simmering point. Heat the butter in a large frying pan. Remove the crusts from the bread slices and cut slices in half. When the butter is very hot, slip in the bread and fry until golden brown on both sides.

Put two pieces of the bread into each of four heated soup bowls and sprinkle with a little Parmesan cheese. Gently crack the eggs on top of the bread, season with salt and pepper and sprinkle with the remaining cheese. Slowly pour over the simmering stock, being careful not to break the egg yolks. Serve immediately.

Risi è Bisi

Rice and peas is the most aristocratic of rice dishes; it was served every year at the Doge's banquets on 25 April, on the feast of San Marco, when the first young peas, grown on the islands of the Venetian lagoon, appear in the market.

Risi e Bisi is served as a soup. It should be runny enough to be eaten with a spoon.

½ small onion, very finely chopped
2 oz/50 g/¼ cup butter
2 tbsp chopped parsley, preferably flat-leaved
10 oz/300 g/1¼ cup fresh peas, shelled weight, or frozen
petits pois, thawed
1¾ pt/1 litre/4 cups homemade stock
12 oz/350 g/1½ cups Italian rice
salt and freshly ground black pepper
5 tbsp freshly grated Parmesan cheese

Put the onion and half the butter in a heavy saucepan and sauté until the onion is pale golden and soft. Mix in the peas and half the parsley and cook over a low heat for 5 minutes if you are using fresh peas, 1 to 2 minutes if using frozen. Add a few tablespoons of stock if necessary.

Meanwhile bring the stock to the boil. Pour the stock over the peas, bring the stock to the boil again and mix in the rice. Cover the pan and cook, over a low heat, until the rice is cooked, stirring occasionally. Taste and adjust seasonings. Remove from the heat and mix in the remaining butter, the rest of the parsley and the Parmesan cheese. Mix well and serve immediately.

Risotto alla Milanese

Risotto with saffron is the only risotto that in Italy is served as an accompaniment. It is eaten with ossobuco (see page 50) and with breaded veal chops. It is also delicious on its own as a first course. If you cannot find beef marrow, use unsmoked streaky bacon. For a real risotto you must use Italian rice.

---

1 ¾ pints/1 litre/4 cups homemade meat stock or 2 bouillon
cubes dissolved in the same amount of water
1 shallot or ½ small onion, finely chopped
1 oz/25 g/2 tbsp beef marrow
2 oz/50 g/6 tbsp butter
12 oz/350 g/1 ½ cups arborio rice, or other Italian rice
3 fl oz/75 ml/⅓ cup dry red wine
⅓ tsp powdered saffron or 2 pinches saffron strands
salt and pepper
2 oz/50 g/½ cup freshly grated Parmesan cheese

Heat the stock to a low simmering point and keep it simmering. Put the shallot, beef marrow and 1 oz/25 g/2 tbsp of the butter in a saucepan, sauté until the shallot is soft and translucent, and then add the rice. Cook, stirring, until the rice is well coated with fat, about 1 to 2 minutes. Pour in the wine, boil for 2 minutes, stirring constantly, and then pour in 7 fl oz/200 ml/¾ cup of stock. Cook at a steady simmer until nearly all the stock has been absorbed and then add another 7 fl oz of stock, and so on. About halfway through the cooking (risotto takes about 25 to 30 minutes to cook) add the saffron dissolved in a little stock. When the rice is ready – it should be soft and creamy, not mushy or runny – taste and adjust the seasoning.

Remove from the heat and mix in the rest of the butter and 2 tablespoons of the cheese. Serve immediately, handing round the rest of the cheese separately.

Spaghetti alla Carbonara

The creation of this dish is attributed to the *carbonari* – charcoal burners – who used to make charcoal in the mountainous forests of Lazio. Traditionally, the meat used was the jowl of the pig, but nowadays most carbonara is made with pancetta, which is belly of pork, similar to streaky bacon but differently cured.

---

1 tbsp olive oil
4 sage leaves, 1 clove garlic
4 oz/125 g smoked pancetta or smoked streaky bacon, cut into matchsticks

12 oz/350 g spaghetti	*salt and freshly ground black*
3 eggs	*pepper*
5 tbsp freshly grated	*2 oz/50 g/4 tbsp butter*
Parmesan cheese	

Heat the oil, sage and whole garlic clove in a large frying pan and add the bacon. Sauté for about 10 minutes, until the bacon is golden brown. Discard the garlic and the sage. Drop the spaghetti into rapidly boiling salted water and cook until *al dente*, firm to the bite. Meanwhile lightly beat the eggs and combine with the cheese, salt and a generous amount of black pepper. Drain the pasta reserving 1 cupful of the water. Return the spaghetti to the saucepan and toss with the butter, then add it to the bacon in the frying pan. Stir-fry for a minute or so, then transfer to a heated bowl. Pour the egg and cheese mixture over the pasta and add about 4 tablespoons of the reserved water to give the sauce the right fluidity. Mix well and serve at once.

Pasta con le Sarde

Pasta with fresh sardines from Sicily is like a history of that island in microcosm: part Greek, part Saracen, part Norman. If you cannot obtain wild or cultivated fennel leaves, use a small fennel bulb cut into strips, together with its feathery green top. If fresh sardines are not available, use sprats.

2 oz/50 g/¼ cup sultanas	3 anchovy fillets, chopped
3 fl oz/75 ml/5 tbsp olive oil	1 lb/450 g fresh sardines,
salt	filleted
1 onion, very finely sliced	1 tsp fennel seed
2 oz/50 g pine nuts	freshly ground black pepper
2 oz/50 g fennel leaves	12 oz/350 g penne or rigatoni

Soak the sultanas in warm water for 10 minutes. Drain and dry well with kitchen paper. Put 3 tablespoons of the oil in a frying pan, add the onion and salt and sauté gently for 10 minutes, stirring frequently, until onion is soft. Mix in the sultanas and pine nuts and cook for a further 2 minutes. Meanwhile blanch the fennel leaves for 1 minute (if using fennel bulb, cook it until soft). Remove fennel from the water, drain and dry. Reserve the cooking water. Chop the fennel and add it and the anchovy fillets to the onion mixture. Cook slowly for 10 to 15 minutes, adding fennel water whenever the mixture begins to dry out. Chop about half the sardines and add to the pan with the fennel seeds and a generous grinding of pepper. Cook for 10 minutes, stirring frequently and adding water when necessary. Adjust seasoning. Meanwhile cook the pasta in the fennel water until *al dente*. Drain, return the pasta to the pan and dress immediately with the sardine sauce. Grease a deep ovenproof dish with a little oil and transfer the pasta into it. Lay the remaining sardines over the pasta, dribble with the rest of the oil and cover with aluminium foil. Bake in a preheated oven at gas mark 6, 400°F, 200°C for 15 minutes.

This dish can be prepared a few hours in advance and then baked for an extra 10 minutes to heat the pasta through. It must be eaten on the same day.

Vermicelli al Sugo

In Italy every cook has his or her favourite recipe for making a sugo, or tomato sauce, for the pasta. This is the one I use when local fresh tomatoes are not in season.

---

5 tbsp extra virgin olive oil
2 oz/50 g/4 tbsp very finely chopped onions
1½ lb/700 g/3 cups canned Italian plum tomatoes, coarsely chopped, with their juice
1 tbsp tomato purée
salt and freshly ground black pepper
12 oz/350 g vermicelli (thin spaghetti)
2 tsp dried oregano   freshly grated Parmesan cheese

Heat the oil in a heavy saucepan. Cook the onion over a moderate heat for 7 to 8 minutes, until it is soft but not browned. Add the tomatoes, tomato purée and seasoning. Simmer uncovered for about 40 minutes, stirring occasionally, and adding water if necessary. Press the sauce through a fine sieve or a food mill into a pan. Its consistency should be fairly thick. Adjust seasoning. Keep warm while you cook the pasta.

Bring 7 pints/4 litres/4 quarts of water to the boil. Add 1½ tablespoons of salt and when the water is boiling fast add the vermicelli, pushing it down gently into the water as it becomes soft. Cook until *al dente* and then drain it. Never overdrain pasta; just give the colander a jerk or two. Transfer pasta to a heated bowl into which you have put 2 tablespoons of the hot sauce. Spoon over the remaining sauce, toss thoroughly and sprinkle with the oregano. Serve immediately, handing round the Parmesan separately.

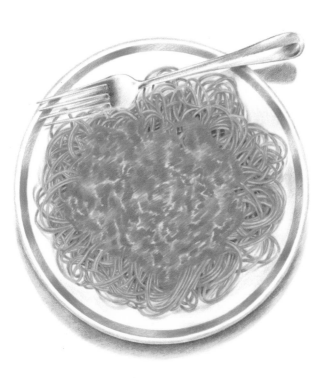

Lasagne al Forno

Emilia-Romagna is the motherland of homemade pasta, where this popular dish was created. Lasagne al forno is a rich dish typical of the region and its food-loving inhabitants. The bolognese sauce is also excellent for dressing tagliatelle or penne.

---

1 lb/500 g fresh lasagne or 10 oz/300 g dried lasagne
3 oz/75 g/¾ cup freshly grated Parmesan cheese
½ oz/15 g/1 tbsp butter
béchamel sauce made with 1¼ pt/750 ml/3 cups milk,
3 oz/75 g/6 tbsp butter and 2½ oz/65 g/½ cup flour flavoured
with 2 pinches of grated nutmeg
Bolognese Sauce
1 oz/25 g/2 tbsp butter, 3 tbsp olive oil
2 oz/50 g pancetta or unsmoked streaky bacon
1 small onion, 1 small carrot, 1 small celery stick, 1 small garlic clove, all finely chopped
1 bay leaf, 1½ tbsp tomato purée
10 oz/300 g best minced (ground) beef
¼ pt/125 ml/¾ cup dry white wine
¼ pt/125 ml/¾ cup meat stock
salt and freshly ground black pepper

First make the bolognese sauce. Heat the butter and oil in a saucepan and cook the pancetta for 1 minute. Add the onion and, when it begins to soften, add the carrot, celery, garlic and bay leaf. Stir and cook for 2 minutes. Add the tomato purée and cook over a low heat for 30 seconds. Add the beef and cook briskly until the meat changes colour. Add the wine and boil until the liquid has almost evaporated. Discard the bay leaf and pour in the stock. Mix well, season and simmer uncovered for about 1 hour, adding more water if the sauce becomes too dry. Check seasoning. While the bolognese is cooking, make the béchamel sauce and set aside.

Cook the lasagne in plenty of boiling salted water in batches of 5 or 6 sheets at a time. When they are cooked lift them out and plunge them into a bowl of cold water. Remove and pat dry with kitchen paper. Butter a 12 inch x 8 inch/30 cm x 20 cm ovenproof dish. Spread 2 tablespoons of the bolognese sauce on the bottom. Cover with a layer of lasagne, then spread over 2 tablespoons or so of bolognese and the same of béchamel sauce. Sprinkle with a little Parmesan cheese and repeat, building up the dish in layers, ending with a top layer of béchamel sauce.

Dot with butter and bake at gas mark 7, 425°F, 220°C, for 20 minutes. Remove from the oven at least 5 minutes before serving to allow the flavours to develop.

Trenette al Pesto

The best basil grows in Liguria, and it is there that this heavenly sauce was created to dress the local tagliatelle, which is called trenette. You can also use pesto to dress potato gnocchi (page 21) or steamed new potatoes, or you can add 1 tablespoon to flavour a vegetable soup. When basil is in season, prepare some extra pesto for the freezer. Do not mix in the cheese at this stage; add it when you use the sauce.

---

1 lb/500 g fresh tagliatelle or 12 oz/350 g dried egg tagliatelle
1 oz/25 g/2 tbsp butter
Pesto
2 oz/50 g/1 cup fresh basil leaves
1 oz/25 g/2 tbsp pine nuts
2 garlic cloves
¼ pt/120 ml/½ cup extra virgin olive oil
4 tbsp freshly grated Parmesan cheese
2 tbsp freshly grated pecorino cheese
salt and freshly ground black pepper

Pesto Put the basil, pine nuts, garlic and oil in a food processor or blender and process until evenly blended. Stop once or twice and scrape the mixture down from the sides of the bowl. Transfer to a large bowl and mix in the cheeses. Season to taste.

Cook the tagliatelle in plenty of boiling salted water. Scoop out a cupful of the water in which the pasta is boiling and set aside. Drain the pasta (do not overdrain) and transfer immediately to the bowl of pesto. Add the butter and toss thoroughly, adding some of the pasta water to give the pasta the correct fluidity. Serve at once.

Gnocchi di Patate

These are the most popular kind of gnocchi. The best ways to dress them are with melted butter flavoured with sage and garlic, with pesto (page 18) or with tomato sauce (page 14).

1¾ lb/800 g floury potatoes, all about the same size
1 egg
5 oz/150 g/1¼ cups strong white flour
salt, 1 tbsp olive oil or sunflower oil

Cook the potatoes in their skins. Drain and peel them as soon as they are cool enough to handle. Purée them through a food mill or a potato ricer. Make a well in the middle, beat the egg lightly with a fork and add to the potato purée. Work in about half the flour and 1 teaspoon salt. Knead and add more flour until the mixture no longer sticks to your hands. It should be soft, smooth and slightly sticky. Knead for a further 2 minutes. With floured hands break off portions of the dough and form sausage-like rolls about 1 inch (2½ cm) thick. Cut the rolls into 1 inch (2½ cm) lengths. Dust each dumpling lightly with flour and press it lightly against the inner side of the prongs of a fork with a quick downward movement. Lay the gnocchi on trays covered with kitchen cloths. Chill in the refrigerator for 30 minutes or longer. Cook in three batches in plenty of boiling water to which you have added the oil and one tablespoon of salt. The gnocchi will soon come to the surface. Cook them for a further minute or so and then retrieve them. Pat dry with kitchen paper. Spoon over a little of whichever sauce you have chosen and keep warm. Toss gently and serve.

Pizza alla Napoletana

Today pizzas have many different toppings. I am a purist: I like my pizza to be covered with the traditional topping – simply tomatoes, oregano and olive oil. Here is my recipe.

---

15 g / ½ oz / 1 tbsp fresh yeast   1 tbsp salt
200 g / 7 oz / 2 cups strong flour   1½ tbsp extra virgin olive oil
Topping
3 tbsp extra virgin olive oil
350 g / 12 oz / 1½ cups chopped canned tomatoes, without juice
1 tsp oregano
1 large clove garlic, peeled and very thinly sliced
salt and freshly ground black pepper
(serves 2 or 3)

Dissolve the yeast in about 6 tablespoons of warm water. Leave aside for 10 minutes. Put the flour on a working surface and make a well in its centre. Add salt, dissolved yeast and oil. Work into a ball, adding a little more water if necessary. Place in a floured bowl, cover with a thick cloth and leave to rise in a warm place for about 2 hours. You can make the dough in a food processor. For the topping, cook the tomatoes and a little salt in 1 tablespoon of olive oil. Cook for about 5 minutes on a high heat. Preheat an oven tray in the oven at gas mark 7, 425°F, 220°C. Knock back and roll it out into an 8 inch (20 cm) diameter disc and place on the heated and floured oven tray. Spoon the tomato sauce over, sprinkle with

oregano and garlic and season. Dribble with the remaining olive oil. Bake for 15 minutes until the rim is gold and the pizza is cooked through. Serve immediately.

Polenta

'A harvest moon in a large circle of mist' is how the 19th-century novelist and poet Alessandro Manzoni described this most homely dish from northern Italy. I always make more than I need for one meal. The next day I serve it grilled as an accompaniment to any sort of meat or fish, or I bake it in slices, layered with bolognese sauce and béchamel sauce just like lasagne.

---

10 oz/300 g/2¼ cups coarse-ground maize (corn meal)
1 tbsp salt

Fill a large deep and heavy saucepan with 2½ pints/1½ litres/6 cups of water. Heat and when the water boils add the salt. Turn the heat down and add the flour in a very thin stream, stirring constantly. Cook, stirring constantly for the first 10 minutes and then every minute or so for at least 40 minutes. When done, turn the polenta onto a board or dish and serve either with your favourite rich stew, with Manzo Brasato (page 49) or with plenty of butter and ½ lb/200 g of creamy Gorgonzola cheese.

To make polenta in the oven, boil the maize flour and water for 2 minutes, stirring constantly. Pour into a buttered oven dish and bake for 1 hour at gas mark 5, 375°F, 190°C.

Grilled Polenta
Cook the polenta as above, and spread it out on a dish or board to a thickness of about 2 inches (5 cm). When cool, cut into ½ inch (1 cm) slices. Brush slices with olive oil and grill on both sides until a crust forms. Sliced polenta is also excellent fried in butter or olive oil.

Radicchio alla Trevisana

In Veneto, radicchio is traditionally grilled as in this recipe. If you cannot find radicchio, Little Gem lettuces or Belgian chicory are good substitutes. Radicchio can be barbecued in the same way.

---

4 radicchio heads, weighing about 1¾ lb/800 g
6 tbsp extra virgin olive oil
salt
freshly ground black pepper

Heat the grill. Discard the bruised outside leaves of the radicchio heads, cut the heads into wedges, wash and dry thoroughly. Place the radicchio in the grill pan, spoon the oil over them and season with salt and a generous amount of pepper. Grill for about 7 minutes, turning the wedges over halfway through cooking. Turn the heat down if the radicchio begins to scorch. Transfer the radicchio to a dish and spoon over the juice from the grill pan. Serve hot or cold as an accompaniment to roast meat, as a first course or as a second course for a simple supper.

Panzanella

This is a traditional rustic summer salad from Tuscany made with country bread and raw vegetables. It is usually served as a first course.

---

8 slices good quality white bread, one day old
12 fresh basil leaves, coarsely torn
1 clove garlic, peeled and chopped
½ cucumber, peeled and cut into ½ inch (1 cm) slices
½ red onion or other sweet onion, sliced
8 oz/225 g ripe meaty tomatoes, either plum or beefsteak,
seeded and cut into ½ inch (1 cm) cubes
salt and freshly ground black pepper
5 tbsp extra virgin olive oil
1 tbsp wine vinegar

Soak the bread in cold water until just soft, then squeeze out all the water and put the bread in a salad bowl. The bread should be damp but not wet. Add the basil, garlic, vegetables and salt and pepper. Toss thoroughly with the oil, using a fork, and chill for 30 minutes or so. Add the vinegar just before serving.

Insalata Caprese

The Italian name of this recipe – salad from Capri – underlines the importance of the ingredients: sound, ripe tomatoes, fresh basil, and mozzarella made from buffalo's milk such as you find on the island. Buffalo mozzarella is tastier and milkier than that made from cow's milk. It is available in the best Italian delicatessens, but if you cannot find it, use Italian mozzarella packed in its whey.

This is a very attractive and fresh first course.

---

4 beefsteak tomatoes
2 Italian mozzarellas, about 8 oz/250 g
1 small bunch of fresh basil
5 tbsp extra virgin olive oil
salt and freshly ground black pepper
4 oz/125 g/½ cup black olives
½ clove garlic, optional

Wash and dry the tomatoes. Slice them thickly and lay the slices on a dish, slightly overlapped. Slice the mozzarella and tuck slices alternately between the tomato slices. Tear up the basil leaves and sprinkle over the salad. Pour the oil over and season. Decorate with the olives. If you like raw garlic, chop some finely and sprinkle over the salad.

Peperoni Arrostiti in Insalata

Peppers that are roasted and then peeled taste quite different from raw peppers. They are perfect either by themselves, or as part of an antipasto or as an accompaniment to roast meats.

4 yellow and red peppers	2 tbsp chopped parsley
4 tbsp extra virgin olive oil	salt and pepper
1 clove garlic, chopped	2 oz/50 g anchovy fillets

Place the peppers under a preheated grill or on a wire rack directly over a gas flame. Cook, turning, until the skin is charred black all over. Peel off the burnt skin, using a small knife, and gently wipe the peppers with kitchen paper. Cut each pepper into quarters, remove and discard the seeds and white ribs and cut into thin strips. Put the oil in a bowl, add garlic, parsley, salt and pepper. Pound the anchovy fillets and mix into the oil mixture.

Arrange the strips of peppers in a dish and spoon the sauce over them. Allow to stand for at least 30 minutes before serving.

Verdure alla Contadina

This is the stewed vegetable dish that in Emilia-Romagna is traditionally served with Pollo alla Cacciatora.

---

3 tbsp olive oil
2 oz/50 g pancetta or smoked streaky bacon, chopped
2 medium-sized onions, sliced
3 medium-sized waxy potatoes, cubed
2 meaty yellow peppers, cut into small pieces
8 oz/250 g fresh ripe tomatoes, peeled
salt and pepper

Heat the oil, the pancetta and the onions in a heavy saucepan. Cook gently until the onions are soft, then add the potatoes. Cook for 5 minutes, turning the potato cubes constantly. Add the peppers and continue cooking for 5 minutes, then add the tomatoes. Season and cover the pan. Cook over a low heat until the potatoes are tender. Add one or two tablespoons of stock or water whenever the dish becomes too dry. Serve hot or warm.

Cacciucco

There are many ways to prepare a good cacciucco, but it always needs chilli and a variety of fresh fish. The people of Leghorn, in Tuscany, say that it should have at least five different kinds of fish, one for each 'c' in cacciucco.

3¼ lb/1½ kg fish (selection of red mullet, squid, hake, whiting, rascasse, John Dory, conger or moray eel, monkfish), 1 bay leaf, salt, 1 pint/500 g mussels, 6 king prawns
1 tbsp wine vinegar
¼ pt/150 ml/⅔ cup extra virgin olive oil
1 onion, 1 small celery stick, 2 cloves garlic, all very finely chopped
1 dried chilli, chopped, 3 tbsp chopped parsley
14 oz/400 g/2 cups tinned plum tomatoes, coarsely chopped
¼ pint/150 ml/⅔ cup dry white wine
freshly ground pepper
8 slices of toasted French bread, rubbed with garlic
(serves 6)

To make fish stock, put all the heads, tails and fins of the fish in a saucepan. Cover with about 1¾ pints/1 litre/4 cups of cold water, add the bay leaf, a very little salt and simmer for 20 minutes. Strain the fish stock into a clean saucepan. Meanwhile scrub the mussels under cold water and remove any barnacles and beard with a sharp knife. Discard any mussels that remain open when knocked against a hard surface. Clean the squid and cut the sacs into strips and the tentacles into pieces. Cut the other fish into chunks.

Sauté gently the onion, garlic, celery, chilli and half the parsley in oil in a large heavy pan for 10 minutes. Add squid and sauté for a further 10 minutes, stirring frequently. Add tomatoes and a little salt. Cook over moderate heat for 10 minutes and then add wine. Boil briskly for 2 to 3 minutes. Add all the other fish except the seafood, cook for 5 minutes, stirring very frequently, and cover with about 1 pint/ ½ litre/2 cups of hot fish stock. Cover pan and simmer for 20 minutes. Add the mussels and cook for 1 minute, until they are open. Add the prawns and remaining parsley and cook for a further minute or so. Adjust seasoning. Put 2 slices of the toasted bread in each soup bowl and ladle the stew over it.

Sepie in Tecia

This dish is made with cuttlefish in Venice, its place of origin, but those delicious creatures can be difficult to find. You can use the more easily available squid, as I do, very successfully.

2 lb/1 kg cuttlefish or squid	2 cloves garlic, sliced
6 tbsp olive oil	4 fl oz/125 ml dry white wine
bunch of parsley, chopped	salt and pepper

Clean the cuttlefish or squid, reserving 3 or 4 ink sacs. Cut the prepared cuttlefish bodies into strips about 1 cm (½ inch) wide, and the tentacles into small pieces. Heat the oil with the parsley and garlic in a heavy pan. This mixture is called soffritto. Add the cuttlefish and coat in the soffritto for 5 to 10 minutes, stirring frequently. Turn the heat up and splash with the wine. Bring to the boil. Add the ink sacs, a good grinding of pepper and salt. Stir well and cover the pan. Cook very gently until the cuttlefish are very tender – at least 1 hour. Squid, especially small ones, will take less time – about 40 minutes. They are cooked when they can easily be pierced by the prong of a fork. If the juice is too watery at the end of cooking, transfer the cuttlefish to a heated serving bowl and reduce the juices briskly until rich and tasty. Check seasonings. Serve with grilled polenta or with boiled rice.

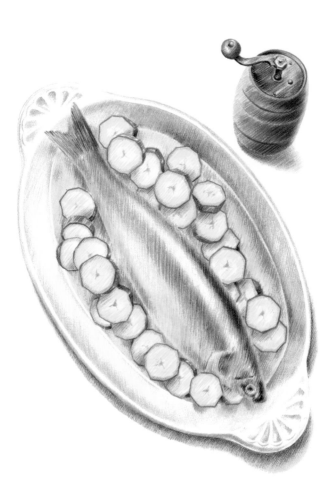

Cefalo con le Zucchine

Grey mullet is an excellent fish, and cheap. See that all the scales have been removed, but leave the head and tail on. The fish looks more attractive this way, and the head gives it a stronger flavour.

---

1 lb/500 g courgettes
salt
6 tbsp extra virgin olive oil
freshly ground black pepper
1½ tbsp oregano
1 grey mullet, about 2-2½ lb/1 kg, prepared

Cut the courgettes into ¼ inch (½ cm) rounds, put them in a colander and sprinkle with salt. Leave to sweat for 30 minutes, then dry very thoroughly with kitchen paper. Transfer to a bowl. Pour the oil into a small bowl and add plenty of pepper and the oregano. Beat well with a fork. Wash and clean the fish under running water and dry thoroughly. Season inside and out with salt and lay it in an oiled roasting tin. Pat half of the oregano mixture on each side of the fish. Add the rest to the courgettes and toss them well. Spoon them around the fish. Cover the tin with foil and bake for 15 minutes at gas mark 5, 375°F, 190°C. Remove the foil, baste, turn the courgettes over and cook, uncovered, until fish is done, a further 15 to 20 minutes.

Transfer the fish carefully to a heated dish and surround it with the courgettes. Spoon the cooking juices over the fish and serve at once.

Zuppa di Muscoli

Although it is called a soup, this dish consists of mussels served in the cooking juices. It is always eaten as a first course.

4 lb / 1 ¾ kg mussels	¼ pt / 150 ml / ⅔ cup dry white
4 fl oz / 120 ml olive oil	wine
2 cloves garlic, peeled and very	1 tbsp lemon juice
thickly sliced	freshly ground black pepper
4 tbsp chopped parsley	toasted slices of French bread

Put the mussels in a sink of cold water. Scrub them with a stiff brush and remove barnacles and beards. Discard any mussels that remain open when knocked against a hard surface. Rinse thoroughly under cold water. Heat the oil, garlic, and 3 tablespoons of the parsley in a large frying pan. After 1 minute splash in the wine and let it bubble for 30 seconds or so to evaporate the alcohol. Add the mussels, cover and cook over a medium heat for about 2 minutes, shaking the pan very frequently. Transfer mussels as they open to a bowl. Keep them warm while you continue cooking the remainder. When all the mussels are removed, filter the cooking liquid through a sieve lined with cheesecloth into a small bowl and mix in the lemon juice. Taste, add salt if necessary and plenty of black pepper. Put 2 or 3 slices of toasted bread into 4 individual bowls and cover with a ladleful of the mussels. Pour over the liquid and sprinkle with remaining parsley. Serve at once.

Arista alla Fiorentina

The name of this ancient dish has its origin in an event that took place in 1430. When this roast was served in Florence at the ecumenical council of Roman and Greek churches, one of the Greek bishops, on tasting the pork, exclaimed 'Aristos, aristos!' – 'The best!' And so it is.

---

2 cloves garlic, peeled and finely chopped
2 rosemary sprigs, about 3½ inches (10 cm) long or 1½ tsp dried rosemary
salt and freshly ground black pepper
2-2½ lb/1 kg boned loin of pork, rindless
2 cloves
3 tbsp olive oil
(serves 6)

Chop together the garlic and the rosemary, add salt and pepper and mix well. Make small incisions in the joint and push a little of the mixture into the meat. Pat the rest all over the meat and stick in the cloves. Rub with half the oil. Allow to stand for a few hours in a cool place. Put the rest of the oil with the meat in a roasting tin. Roast in a preheated oven at gas mark 4, 350°F, 180°C until quite tender, about 1½ hours, basting and turning the joint every 20 minutes. Turn the oven up to gas mark 7, 425°F, 220°C for the last 10 minutes to brown the meat. Transfer meat onto a wooden board. Remove fat from the cooking liquid. Add 4 tablespoons of hot water and boil briskly while loosening the residue at the bottom of the pan. Carve the meat , spoon the cooking juices over it and serve. This roast is equally succulent and delicious served cold.

Castratello alla Cacciatora

This dish of lamb, pot-roasted with vinegar, is made, with slight variations, all over central Italy.

---

2 tbsp fresh rosemary needles, chopped or 2 tsp dried rosemary
2 cloves garlic, peeled and finely chopped
salt and freshly ground black pepper
3¼ lb / 1½ kg leg of lamb
3 tbsp olive oil
1 small onion, very finely chopped
4 fl oz / 120 ml / ½ cup red wine vinegar
4 juniper berries, bruised, 4 anchovy fillets
freshly ground black pepper
(serves 6)

Mix together the rosemary, garlic, salt and pepper. Make a few deep incisions in the lamb and push in pinches of this mixture. Heat the oil with the onion in a casserole just big enough to hold the lamb. Add a pinch of salt and sauté the onion gently until soft but not brown. Add the meat and brown gently on all sides, then add the vinegar and juniper berries. Boil briskly for 2 minutes, then add 4 fl oz / 120 ml / ½ cup of boiling water. Season generously with pepper, and cook, covered, at a very low heat until the meat is tender, about 2 hours. Turn the meat over a few times during cooking. Remove the meat and allow to stand for a few minutes. Meanwhile, if necessary, reduce the cooking juices until they are rich and syrupy, and adjust seasonings. Chop the anchovy fillets finely and mix into the juices. Boil gently for 1 minute. Carve the lamb and serve accompanied by the sauce.

Manzo Brasato al Barolo

In this classic recipe for braised beef from Piedmont, the wine used is the renowned Barolo, but any good, full-bodied red wine will do. Barolo, with white truffles, is one of the glories of the region. This dish is traditionally served with polenta. Porcini (cep) are wild mushrooms which can be bought in the best supermarkets or any Italian specialist shops; they are essential in this recipe.

---

3 lb/1¼ kg chuck steak or eye of the shoulderblade, in one
piece, securely tied
2 tbsp flour, 4 tbsp olive oil

Marinade

1 bottle Barolo wine	1 tbsp peppercorns, ground
⅓ oz/10 g dried porcini	in a mortar
2 carrots, cut into pieces	1 sprig rosemary
2 onions, quartered	2 bay leaves
4 celery sticks, cut in chunks	pinch of cinnamon
3 cloves	salt

(serves 6)

Put the beef in a large bowl. Add the mixed marinade ingredients, cover with cling film and marinate for 24 hours. Remove the meat from the marinade and dry very thoroughly with kitchen paper. Mix 1 teaspoon of salt with a couple of tablespoons of flour and coat the meat lightly with the mixture. Heat the oil in an earthenware pot or cast-iron casserole. Add the beef and brown on all sides. Heat the marinade to boiling point and pour over the meat. Cover the pot and cook in the oven at gas mark 3, 325°F, 170°C, for 2½ hours or until the meat is very tender. Turn the meat every 30 minutes. When cooked, remove beef from the pot, cover with foil and keep it warm. Pour the liquid and vegetables into a blender and process until smooth. Reheat in a saucepan, checking the seasoning. Carve the beef into ¼ inch (½ cm) slices and serve coated with a little sauce. Serve the rest of the sauce separately to dress the polenta or buttery mashed potatoes.

Ossobuco

Ossobuco is a cut from the middle of the hind leg of a calf, and is referred to as shank by some butchers. During cooking, the gelatinous substance in the meat of the shin melts into the cooking juices, making them rich, tasty and thick. When eating ossobuco, don't forget to scoop out the marrow from the bone; it is delicious.

---

1 tbsp olive oil
2 oz/50 g/4 tbsp butter
2 onions, 1 carrot, 1 stick celery, ½ clove garlic,
all finely chopped
4 ossobuco
4 tbsp flour
salt and freshly ground black pepper
4 fl oz/125 ml/½ cup dry white wine
8 oz/225 g/1 cup canned plum tomatoes, coarsely chopped
½ pint/300 ml/1¼ cups meat stock or 1 chicken bouillon cube
dissolved in the same quantity of water

Gremolada Sauce

| 1 tsp grated lemon rind | ½ clove garlic, very finely |
| 1 tbsp chopped parsley | chopped |

Put the oil, butter, onion, carrot, celery and garlic in a sauté pan large enough to contain all the ossobuco in a single layer. Sauté for about 10 minutes. Meanwhile tie each ossobuco as you would a parcel. Lightly coat in seasoned flour. When the vegetables are soft, push them to one side of the pan and brown the meat well on all sides. Pour in the wine and boil it rapidly for about 2 minutes,

turning the veal several times. Add the tomatoes, their juice, half the stock and a little salt and pepper. Cover and cook over very low heat for 2 hours, until the meat begins to come away from the bone. Turn and baste the ossobuco four or five times during the cooking. Do this with great care to prevent the marrow falling out. If the final sauce is too thin, remove the veal and reduce the sauce briskly. Adjust seasoning. Mix the lemon rind, garlic and parsley to make the gremolada and spoon the mixture into the pan containing the meat and sauce. Cook for about a minute and then transfer ossobuco to a heated dish. Remove the string and pour the sauce over the meat. Serve at once with risotto alla milanese (page 9).

Pollo alla Cacciatora

Chicken is cooked in all regions of central Italy, in many different versions. This version is from Emilia-Romagna, where it is often served with stewed vegetables (page 34), an ideal partnership.

---

1 oz/25 g dried porcini mushrooms
2 tbsp olive oil
4 oz/125 g onion, finely chopped
1 celery stalk, chopped
4 oz/125 g pancetta or unsmoked streaky bacon
3 lb/1¼ kg chicken, cut into small joints
¼ pt/150 ml/⅔ cup dry white wine
8 oz/250 g/1 cup canned plum tomatoes with their juice
salt and freshly ground black pepper

Soak the porcini in a cupful of hot water for 30 minutes. Drain into a bowl, filter the liquid through a piece of muslin and reserve. Rinse the porcini under cold water and dry thoroughly. Cut into small pieces. Sauté the onion in the oil for 10 minutes. Add the celery and cook for a further 5 minutes, stirring often. Remove the vegetables and set aside. Cook the pancetta in the pan over low heat for 2 or 3 minutes. Add the chicken joints and sauté on all sides until they are a pale golden colour. Turn up the heat and splash in the wine. Let it bubble away and add the tomatoes, the porcini with their filtered liquid and salt and pepper. Return the vegetables to the pot. Cook, uncovered, over a low heat until the chicken is cooked. Transfer the chicken to a heated dish, adjust the seasoning and, if necessary, reduce the sauce. Spoon the sauce over the chicken and serve at once.

Pollo alla Diavola

Tuscan chickens are the best in Italy and they are cooked in the simplest of ways, as in this traditional recipe for devilled chicken.

I young roasting chicken, about 2½ lb/1¼ kg
4 fl oz/120 ml/½ cup extra virgin olive oil
salt and freshly ground black pepper
I lemon, cut into wedges

Split the chicken in half down the backbone. Flatten it gently with a meat pounder, taking care not to splinter the bones. Mix the oil, salt and plenty of milled pepper and brush the chicken all over with the mixture. Heat the grill to a medium heat and place chicken, cut side upwards, about 5 inches (12 cm) away from the heat. Grill for about 15 minutes, then turn chicken over. Baste with more seasoned oil and cook for a further 10 minutes or so, brushing with the seasoned oil from time to time, until chicken is done. The skin should be dark brown and crackly. Serve immediately with a green salad.

Torta di Ricotta

Cakes and puddings made with ricotta cheese are very popular all over central and southern Italy. In some recipes the ricotta mixture is baked in a blind-baked pastry case. Other cooks, myself included, prefer to bake the mixture directly in a tin, to produce a moister and lighter cake. In Italy we serve this torta without cream, but you may like to hand around a jug of pouring cream. It makes a richer pudding for a dinner party.

2 oz/50 g/½ cup sultanas	4 oz/120 g/¾ cup mixed peel
2 tbsp rum	grated rind of I lemon
18 oz/500 g/2½ cups ricotta	grated rind of I orange
4 tbsp double cream	4 large eggs, separated
2 oz/50 g/½ cup flour	2 tbsp dried breadcrumbs
4 oz/120 g/½ cup caster sugar	icing sugar

(serves 6)

Soak the sultanas in rum for at least 30 minutes. Pass the ricotta through a food mill or sieve into a bowl and fold in the cream. Add the flour, sifting it through a fine sieve, and the caster sugar, reserving 1 tablespoon. Mix well. Add the mixed peel, sultanas, grated rind and egg yolks. Mix very thoroughly until the yolks are fully incorporated. Whisk the egg whites until stiff but not dry and fold them into the mixture very lightly, one spoonful at a time. Butter an 8 inch (20 cm) spring-clip cake tin. Mix the breadcrumbs with the reserved tablespoon of sugar and sprinkle them over the tin. Shake the tin until the entire surface is covered with the breadcrumb mixture. Spoon the ricotta mixture into the tin and bake for about 1 hour in a preheated oven at gas mark 4, 350°F, 180°C. The cake shrinks when it is ready, and becomes dry and springy. Leave to cool in the tin, then unmould it and cover with icing sugar.

Macedonia di Frutta

Italians are not much given to making, or eating, sweet courses. They usually end the meal with fruit, but sometimes, for a party, they serve a deliciously scented fruit salad. For special occasions they add a glass of spumante – the Italian champagne.

---

2 dessert apples
1 pear
2 bananas
1 lb/500 g assorted fruit such as peaches, grapes, apricots, cherries, melons, plums
4 large oranges, juice only
1 lemon, juice only
sugar to taste, about 3 oz/90 g/6 tbsp
(serves 6)

Peel the apples, pears and bananas and cut into small pieces. Wash, peel if necessary and stone all the other fruits and cut into suitable pieces. The cherries must be stoned and the grapes cut in half and pitted. Put all the fruit in a bowl. Add the juice of the oranges and lemon and the sugar. Cover with cling film and refrigerate for at least 4 hours. Before serving mix again, taste and check the sugar.

Index